Old NEW CUMNOCK

by

Donald McIver

The Castle in 1960. Biddell's Regal Cinema is on the right

© Donald McIver 1997
First published in the United Kingdom, 1997
By Stenlake Publishing, Unit 16a,
Thistle Business Park North, Cumnock,
Ayrshire, KA18 1EQ
Telephone/fax: 01290 423114

ISBN 1 872074 92 8

MANSFIELD HOUSE, NEW CUMNOCK.

Introduction

New Cumnock grew up around a castle which was sometimes called the Castle of the Black Bog, which stood on the site of the present day Arthur Memorial Church and dated from the 14th Century. The earliest map of the area shows the castle as Kumuck Castle and later Timothy Pont's map shows it as Kumnock.

In 1650 the parish was split in two and the parishes of Old and New Cumnock were created. New Cumnock had a greater land area but was sparsely populated. By 1821 the Castle was derelict and in a ruinous state. However a ruined castle was looked on as ideal building material and many of the older houses in the village may be constructed from its remains.

At one time the whole valley was under water, but as the loch silted up the land that was created was inhabited and the village pushed out further from the shelter of the castle. Small crofts were built but the land was poorly drained and marshy. The land was gradually improved as landowners realised the benefits of draining and liming the soil. A pioneer was Sir Charles Menteith who patented a three draw kiln for turning limestone into fertiliser for spreading on the fields. The remains of one of his kilns can be seen at the site of the limestone quarries behind Mansfield Hall Farm. Another of the kilns can be seen at Craigdullyeart and is dated 1837.

Coal has been sought in the parish for centuries, mainly from outcrops or bell pits. These small pits were dug down into the coal seam and as much coal as possible was dug out before the roof collapsed and the miners started another nearby. The waste from it would be thrown into the collapsed workings of the old one.

In the 1700s commercial mining was started by the Afton Mining Company at Straid on the New Cumnock to Dalmellington road. Mining expanded rapidly and there were soon mines at Auchincross, Bridgend, Coalburn, Craigman, Marchburn and Polquhirter. With the coming of the railway in 1850, the industry grew even more important to the local economy and, in 1863, the Bank Coal Company was formed, followed two years later by the Lanemark Coal Company. Both were taken over by New Cumnock Collieries Ltd in 1909. At the end of World War Two the six remaining collieries of Bank, Bridgend, Burnfoot, Coalburn, Knockshinnoch and Seaforth were nationalised.

In 1847, some Yorkshire iron merchants, convinced by reports from the Houldsworths of Dalmellington that an area of high quality ironstone lay just waiting to be exploited, built an ironworks near to the banks of Connelburn. Coal came from Straid by tramway and iron ore and limestone came from the mines on Brockloch. Houses and offices were built to house the employees (many of whom came from Consett in County Durham) and the area became known in later years as the Furnace Rows. The area has now been opencasted and there are few remains of the works which were offered for sale in 1857 at a loss of £100,000.

Limestone has been important locally both for use as a fertiliser and in mortar. Benston and Mansfield limestone had a peculiar property in that it would bind under water making it invaluable in bridge construction. Other minerals mined locally included antimony, lead, graphite and copper. Clay was used in the many brick and tileworks in the area as well as at the Cumnock Pottery.

As well as its rich industrial heritage, New Cumnock has evidence of inhabitation from the earliest times and ancient burial mounds containing human remains have been found at Polquheys, Meikle Creoch and Polqhuirter. There have been two hoards of coins found in the parish, one lot in 1834 and the other in 1882. No one knows who hid the money or why, but the chances are that whoever did, died or was murdered in the troubled times of the 13th and 14th Centuries. Who knows, there may be more undiscovered hoards out there!

The town has suffered greatly with the passing of its most important industry and many people have drifted away from New Cumnock to find jobs elsewhere.

Pathhead, New Cumnock.

Pathhead in 1905, looking across to the Cross Keys pub which is now demolished. The Mansfield Road leads to Corsencone Hill, still a favourite haunt for walkers. Whisky stills were set up illegally at Corsencone Hill as it was remote and the wind carried the fumes away. The largest still was at Craigdullyeart not far from Craigshiel on the old New Cumnock to Kirkconnel and Sanquhar road. Stories abound. A farmer coming off the hill to Merkland with two casks of whisky on his cart saw an exciseman coming towards him so stopped his cart to load it up with reeds for thatching. The exciseman asked if he had seen anything suspicious that day. The farmer said well he didn't like to klype on a neighbour but he had seen Craigsheil off up the hill up to no good. The exciseman rushed off only to discover Craigsheil in his bed!

Taken from near to Jubilee Cottage, this view shows the Afton Buildings on the middle left and the long building behind is the railway goods depot. The railway opened in stages and got to Auchinleck from Kilmarnock in 1848. Construction was simultaneously being done from Dumfries and the last stretch to be opened was from Auchinleck to New Cumnock. The railway bridge crossing the old toll road just below the Bowes cottage was built by the Vulcan Foundry in Kilmarnock and the girders are stamped with the date 1850. The once busy station closed in 1965 only to be re-opened in 1993.

MANSFIELD VILLAGE NEW CUMNOCK.

Mansfield village in 1910. The large building on the right was at one time a carding mill where wool was made ready for spinning by combing out impurities and straightening the fibres. The village was also known as doon the burn.

Burnbrae looking down into Mansfield with the old Bowes cottage in the middle distance. The cottages seen here are mostly gone now but in recent years many attractive houses have been built in their place.

A 1920s view of the Castle area seen from the church tower. The road seen through the trees on the left led up to the Old Church manse and the garage on the right has been redeveloped. Next to it was, until recently, Trotter's. The original Old Church was beside the Castle and was opened in 1659. It was cruciform in shape and initially had three entrances. Viewing the decaying interior as it stands today it is still not too difficult to imagine the former beauty of this little church. By the late 1820s a larger church was needed and the old church was replaced in 1833 by the present structure. Its bell was removed and is still in use in the present church. The old church was abandoned and today is in a ruinous state.

The Castle — New Cumnock

The Castle, viewed from the Blacksmiths. To the left, behind the wooden shed is one of the twin chimneys for the gas works. The houses on the right of this picture are mostly still intact but the left hand side of this view has changed drastically. McKechnie's Garage replaces the wooden shed and all of the sandstone buildings have been demolished. Only the Glens Bar remains today.

New Cumnock Gas Works circa 1930. Lindsay (on the right) the contractor has reversed the small truck into the shed and has loaded up with coke. This was a by-product of coal gas production. Coal was heated in sealed furnaces and several by-products were collected. Tar and creosote were collected from retorts and the coal gas was drawn off into large gasometers after going through a filtration process to remove further impurities. The gas was then piped through the village and used for lighting and cooking.

Castle, New Cumnock.

78680. J.V.

The Castle, looking towards the railway station circa 1914. The coalman is just delivering to the cottage on the left while on the right Templeton's is having a removal sale. Public fountains, such as the one here, were a common site in many local villages having been provided at a time when many houses had no running water inside. Some were ornate and had designs such as lions heads where the water would spout out. The framework was for resting your pail on as it was filled up. Two such fountains can still be seen in Ochiltree.

Down on the left, in this 1920s view of the Castle, were the Post Office and, just next to the van, Henderson's the grocers. Opposite Hendersons was the Regal Cinema, known fondly as Biddalls. It had a decorative frontage and next door was a cafe.

Just behind the nearest van in this view of the Castle, are the offices of Mr Young the solicitor who lived in Jubilee Cottage. A notice fixed to the radiator says 'Kippers' so the van may have been Sloan Wilson's fish van. At the time of this photograph, circa 1935, the Castle also had a newsagent and McFarlane's butchers. The horse drawn van outside Sanny Gibson's shop may have belonged to McFarlane's.

From the church tower circa 1905. The old police station and sergeant's house is to the left of the horse and cart. Just behind the large tree on the right was the mill, built in 1735. It was used for grinding and bruising corn or wheat for animal feed as well as oatmeal for porridge. The lade or water channel from the water wheel crossed under the main road, through the grounds of the Old Mill Farm and from there to the Nith. The Old Mill Farm was once an inn and belonged to the McKnights at the time of Robert Burns.

Looking from the Afton Bridgend toward the Castle circa 1904. At one point this would have been a turnpike road and tolls would have been charged. The money raised was used for the upkeep of the road and, of course, to provide a profit for the builders. It was the introduction of decent roads which helped to start commercial mining in the area. In the 1700s the Afton Mining Company came and exported the coal via the new New Cumnock to Dalmellington Road which was built by McAdam of Craigengillan. On the other side of the valley at Mansfield, Sir Charles Menteith was mining in the Gargrieve Hill area and the coal sold in Dumfries, Annan and Lochmaben. It was taken away to a stowage site in Sanquhar by a cart and bogey road built specially by Menteith.

The Afton Hotel was owned by the Lind family and stood on the banks of the Nith on the north side of the bridge. Located where it was, it was a very popular hotel but was unfortunately totally consumed by fire in January 1963 and the little that was left was subsequently demolished.

This picture and the one opposite show the devastation caused by the fire which prevented many children from getting to school that morning. Much more fun than any school lesson!

Looking from Afton Bridgend towards the Coupla circa 1905. In the distance on the left the village lamplighter can be seen checking one of the gas lamps. The bridge was a popular meeting place to have a blether when going on or off shift at the mines.

The Sultan at **NEW CUMNOCK**

GChristie

Right: Mick Clark came to New Cumnock shortly after the First World War and his shop was a popular place to pick up the latest gossip and to discuss football. To the right of his shop was Sarah Logan's sweetie shop and on the right was Sanny Gibson's fruit and sweet shop. This photo was taken sometime in the 1920s. The building was demolished in 1994 after being gutted by fire.

The Sanatorium, New Cumnock

Glenafton Sanatorium was in the process of being built when this picture was taken in the early 1900s. It was paid for partly by public subscription. At the time tuberculosis caused the death of over 300 Ayrshire folk per year and the need for a specialist hospital was urgent. Rest and recuperation along with clean air were deemed to be the cure until the arrival, in the 1950s, of the wonder drug Streptomycin. The hospital then became a geriatric unit until its closure. In the 1960s it was demolished and a holiday park now occupies the site.

The kennels, or as it was better known, Boltons Farm. Across the road from the farm was the mortuary for Glenafton Hospital. The driveway at the forefront of this picture led to a large boiler house which heated the hospital and supplied hot water for the laundry which was next to the boiler house. One of the boilermen lived in a cottage nearby. In the 1920s and 30s laundry was transferred to and from the hospital in a small cart pulled by an old grey donkey called Auld Nellie.

Lindsay the contractor's cart on its way to Connel Park with the church tower in the background. The field just behind the cart was known as the Mosswell and belonged to Old Mill Farm. In later years it was filled in with waste material from the local collieries.

Connel Park was built in the 1870s and by the 1900s about 1500 people lived in the 250 houses which comprised eight rows of terraced cottages. This view shows the village looking west along the Dalmellington road. The coal reserves of this part of New Cumnock were relatively untouched till a branch was built from the main railway line in the 1860s. Expansion was rapid and the disparate villages along the Dalmellington road became a thriving community.

Store Corner, Connelpark in the early 1950s. The corner was a popular meeting place as the Co-op was just across the road. The large building on the right in the background belonged to Murray's grocers and across the road from there was Smithfield. The rows in Connel Park were named depending on their location and included New Football Row, Long Row and Railway Terrace.

24

The staff of Connelpark Co-op along with that most important member of staff, the rodent controller. The young man on the left was Mr Ferguson.

Staff at Connel Park Co-op in the early 1900s. The corned beef came from Chicago which, at about the same time, became infamous. Upton Sinclair's book The Jungle exposed the working conditions of the Chicago meat packing yards and his story, which was told through the eyes of a Lithuanian immigrant, described the true horror of the conditions that people had to work in and that animals died in. Reputedly, about 25% of those who read the book became vegetarian!

Knockshinnoch Castle Colliery was a state of the art colliery when production began in the mid 1940s. Sinking of the shaft had begun in December 1939 and, although the pit won a few prizes for its production per man shift, it is better known for being the scene of Britain's most dramatic pit rescue. On 7 September 1950 a peat bog burst through into the workings and trapped 116 men. Thirteen were killed and it took fifty three hours to rescue the remainder. These two views show the engineering workshop as well as a general view of the colliery with the canteen on the left.

The pit bottom. The two sets of hutch rails on the left lead to the shaft bottom where the cages were lowered to raise the full hutches or tubs to the surface. The set at the right brought the empties round from the cages to be taken to the belt conveyors to be re-filled. The opening to the left was the sub station where the pit bottom workers took their piece.

Bank House, New Cumnock.

78677. J.V.

Bank House was owned by the Hyslop family who founded the Bank Coal Company. It made a stark contrast to the much more humble room and kitchens and single ends that their workers had to live in and reflected the wealth that their mines and brickworks had generated. Like the rows, Bank House succumbed to the bulldozer in the 1960s.

At the back of the Crescent at the Bank. Taken sometime in the 1940s, the photo shows a happy group of well dressed and very healthy looking kids. All that remains of the Crescent today is a green field site dotted with rubble.

Furnace Row was named after the Nithsdale Iron Company's failed ironworks. Bank No.2 was just behind the cottages on the left and on the right was Seaforth House, built for the managers.

BANK GLEN, NEW CUMNOCK.

This view shows Bank Glen about 1913. The horse drawn vehicle was probably the Laird o' Banks coach. Bank Church was built in 1898 and demolished in 1961.The closure of the mines and opencasting have meant that little now remains of the small communities scattered along the Dalmellington Road. As the mines were closed, people left their scattered windswept villages and were resettled in the new housing scheme at Bridgend.

With the purchase of the iron works came the collieries that the Nithsdale Iron Company had developed. Coal mining at the Bank was extremely successful and lasted for over 100 years with Bank No.6 closing in 1969. Three shafts were in operation in 1868 and there was a brickworks next to Bank No.1.

For the 116 men trapped underground at Knockshinnoch, it was the old abandoned workings around the Bank which ultimately saved their lives. With Knockshinnoch's shaft blocked, the rescuers came in from Bank No.6 and used abandoned workings to get close to where the survivors were trapped. These workings (only 24 feet away through coal and rock from the trapped men) were full of gas and an elaborate system of ventilation was set up. This wasn't enough to clear the gas and the rescue teams had to wear breathing apparatus to reach the survivors. Extra apparatus was gathered from all over Scotland and the trapped men trained quickly in its use. All were brought out safely.

Bank Brae in the 1940s with Craig Murray's horse drawn delivery van coming round the corner at the bottom of the brae. Opposite the van is the Glen Inn and one of the small whitewashed cottages on the right is the Post Office.

Twilight at the Bank - Front Row just before demolition. Craigmark Stores and the pub are at the far right.

Above: By the 1930s pithead baths were being built in all of the newly developed collieries and in many of those which still had a long working life. These ones were at the Bank.

Left: A common scene in many homes in New Cumnock before the advent of pithead baths. Sometimes with a walk of over two miles back home in typical dreich Ayrshire weather, the miner would be totally soaked to the skin and desperate for a bath and dry clothes. Here his wife is drying them off for the next shift.

Half way up the Bank Brae about 1912. Before safety helmets and battery powered lamps, this was the standard headgear for a miner. The tallow lamp was clipped to your cap. The container was filled with oil and a wick fed into the spout. The light was dim and must have put a great strain on a miner's eyes.

Another of Lindsay's carts with a load of wood on the Boig Road en route to one of the mines between Connelpark and the Hawrunnel. In 1837 there were five carriers in the village, most of whom would have been involved in the carriage of coal as well as agricultural produce to the markets at Cumnock and Ayr.

Burnside village and Burnfoot rows with the chimneys of the Bank pit and brickworks in the background. In the middle of the village can be seen a bus at the turning point. The gardens of the houses were all relatively large and many of the gardeners grew pansies sweet peas and carnations. The brickworks closed in the early 1960s after having turned out millions of bricks over the years. The taller of the chimneys was for the Bank's winding engine, originally steam driven. At one time there were extra boilers used to power a generating plant to provide electricity for the colliery.

Burnfoot's original rows were described in 1913 as being the worst in the county. 234 people lived in only forty one houses, most of which had only a single room. For the whole village there were only six double earth closets (with no doors), no washing facilities and no coal houses for any of the rows. By the 1930s when this picture was taken, conditions had improved, but were still poor.

Burnside was built next to Burnfoot and has also gone. This view shows Burnside Hall in the 1950s.

The bus dates from the early 1920s and is probably pictured at the Knowetop Cottages on the Burnfoot road. Although buses had been about since the dawn of motoring, they really came into their own after the First World War. Many ex-army trucks were converted and companies set up in competition to the railways. Of course, in remote places, such as Burnfoot, they were the first real form of reliable and quick public transport and made the lives of the inhabitants so much easier.

Burnfoot pit's lamp station and workshop area. Here are from left to right: Nashy McCracken, Addy Mcnab, Bob Jess, Harry Burgoyne, Jimmy Hose, Johny Flynn, J Blackwood and Mr Cunningham. Burnfoot survived to be nationalised but closed in the early 1950s.

These two pictures show some of the conditions underground. The miners at the coal face are loading the coal onto scraper pans which led to the conveyor belts. These lead to a railhead where a battery locomotive or rope winding engine would haul the coal (now transferred into hutches) to the pit bottom. The little railway would also be used for transporting miners to and from the coal face. The face could be up to two or three miles from the pit bottom. In the (bad) old days, they would be expected to walk, often in back breaking conditions, in their own time. A shift of eight hours and a walk of two hours each way!

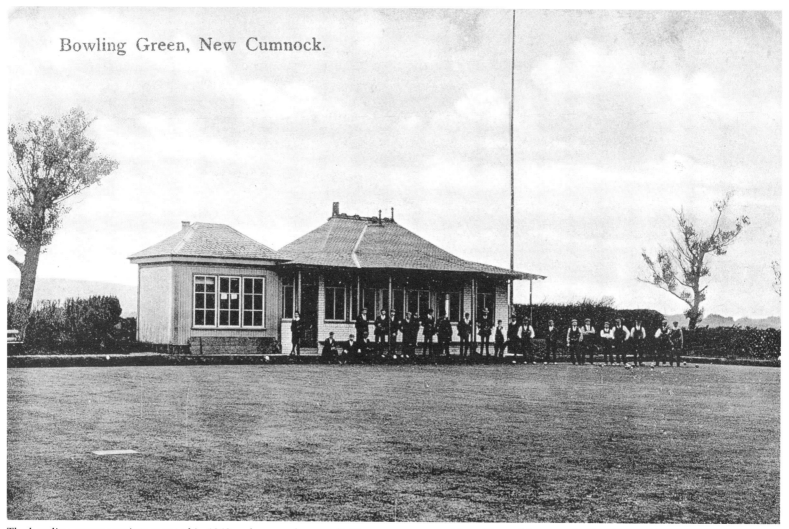

Bowling Green, New Cumnock.

The bowling green was inaugurated in 1860 and was welcome relief for many a weary miner. He could escape the drudgery of his work and play a few ends in the fresh air.

New Cumnock golf clubhouse about 1910. This has been replaced thanks to the old Cumnock & Doon District Council but the club still plays on nine holes. Hopefully, the course will be extended to eighteen holes sometime in the not too distant future.

A gala sometime in the early 1950s. The pipe band was Muirkirk Boys Brigade. The footbridge over the Afton still has to be built and the man leaning on the dyke is at the entrance to the building known as the Old School.

In the first picture is Colin McClatchie in his normal every day clothes and on his way home in 1938. It was often a cold, wet walk home and especially so if your clothes were wet from working down a damp mine. On the right is Colin in his Home Guard uniform. His duty as Sergeant was often done at the end of a long shift and could lead to an all night duty with work again next morning. He served from 1942-45.

A country wedding somewhere in Cumnock & Doon in the 1930s. It may be New Cumnock but it would be nice to hear from anyone in the picture.

Of course, mining wasn't the only activity taking place in the area. Agriculture was also very important and the picture here shows a prize winning Ayrshire coo. The Ayrshire breed was at one time world famous and many thousands have been paid for prize winning stud bulls.

A long gone part of New Cumnock. This early 1900s photo was taken at the entrance to Greenhead Rows (now Mason Avenue). The small cottage on the right was the Findlay home and Mr Watson, the schoolmaster, lived in the building in the centre. The two carts belonged to Lindsay the coal merchant.